Throat Singing

Other books by Susan Cohen

Poetry:

Backstroking (Unfinished Monument Press; 2005)
Finding the Sweet Spot (Finishing Line Press; 2009)

Non-fiction
with Christine Cosgrove:

Normal at Any Cost: Tall Girls, Short Boys, and the Medical Industry's Quest to Manipulate Height (Tarcher/Penguin; 2009)

Throat Singing

Poems by Susan Cohen

Cherry Grove Collections

Published by Cherry Grove Collections
P.O. Box 541106
Cincinnati, OH 45254-1106

ISBN: 9781936370665
LCCN: 2012932832

Poetry Editor: Kevin Walzer
Business Editor: Lori Jareo

Visit us on the web at www.cherry-grove.com

Cover collage by Sarah Loyola
www.loyolaworks.com

Cover photo by Valentino Loyola

To Bob with love

Table of Contents

I. Chamber Music

Throat Singing

he can make his bass
notes rumble with the pulse
of hoof beats on the Steppes

while his larynx also squeezes
the freakish whistle of thin air
heard in the highest passes

and his words ride hard rasping
where have you gone my ponies
where have you gone my country

as he scrapes his hopes together
across the chords
tensed in his throat

but so much straining
as he oscillates the octave
between what he has and what he wants

drives his blood until the veins
leather to reins around his neck
and throat singers die young

with the effort of singing
so many notes at once so much
longing wears out their hearts

Chamber Music

To learn a piece of music
you must get it in your hands.

I was scrambling on my elbows
up the bed, frantic
to back out of maternity.

I see your baby,
the nurse shouted.
Touch its head!

She had to yell until I heard
above the pain.

O, then I reached down
and met his threads of hair,
hot and yolky.

O, then I learned the hard
crescendo of his skull.

Under Trees

An elm crashed down, skidded
across the roof tiles, just missing us
while we slept in a cousin's attic room.

Our acacia full of yellow blossom
missed us as it pitched into the night, shuddering
all the neighborhood dogs awake.
It took two days to chainsaw into logs.

A bay laurel barely missed us, its twiggy
tips clawing our kitchen windows when it dove.

Last month, a silver maple hatcheted
the garage next door, which broke its fall
so that it missed us in broad daylight.

Not one of them gave warning, although finches
probably flew out of the maple limbs.

But after the maple fell, our neighbor said
his lopsided Monterey Pine could topple next.

Every day my eye measures
his huge pine's trajectories: missing us,
just missing us, not missing us.

In a New Jersey summer cottage,
a giant oak stood outside a screened-in porch
where, early every morning, my father wrote.

Something stirred him to a different window
to watch a storm come on.

Seconds later, the thunder of oak,
so much dead weight
clobbering his chair and desk to splinters.

I remember being six and waking early;
the house crammed with branches;
my father in his bathrobe, asking
how much luck someone can have.

As if each person's luck is standing,
waiting to be measured –

if only we could get our arms around
its whole circumference,
embrace its thick, rough trunk.

Lucky Dog

My family bragged during my childhood
   that we owned a dog who smiled.
Mutt of memory, spring-loaded, black-coated,
   when I whistled she came bouncing.

Sometimes she arrived unbidden,
   all unleashed delight. She'd track me
to the school yard, leap to lick my chin,
   knock me flat onto the blacktop.

Suburban evenings on my bike,
   I heard neighbors calling. Their dogs
never came. We had our lucky dog,
   they had sour marriages, dour jobs,

common cancers no one named
   with children present. At the time,
I didn't wonder if our lucky mutt
   was one-part hound, some-part

myth like so much that I was taught
   of happy-ever-after. I just knew
she made me nervous when she pitched
   into my ribs. Already, life

seemed more complex than promised,
   affection excitable and fluid
as a high-voltage tail that sometimes whipped
   across bare legs and stung.

I'd done nothing to deserve
       her generous tongue that slopped
its unrelenting happiness on me, so
       maybe I didn't trust in her,

not fully, not even then.

       That lavish, bounding luck.

That doggy grin.

That Year I Read Anne Frank's Diary

She is my shadow, made of ash
no soap or time will ever wash
away. She shares my observant stare.
Did she have the same trouble with her hair?
She's my age in her last photograph.

I'm thirteen, shy as my buds of breasts,
that year my best friend chooses to confess
I'm the only Jew her mom can bear.
      She's my shadow,

see how tight she clings – first black dress,
soot twin. Why else would my friend ask, not
meaning much: *how many of you are there?*
As if I'm me and others, too. That year
a new girl sits with me in class:
      she's my shadow.

At the Radiation Clinic

On one wall van Gogh's trees twist
from his sun, which tattoos the soil
with their black, orange shadows.
They would run if they could.

Even this cheap print radiates white
and yellow heat to a dozen patients
who have come to respect
the duplicitous power of the x-ray.

My father shuts his eyes, tries dozing
in a wheelchair until his name is called.
I study van Gogh's olive grove,
its sunshine of visible strokes:

How he saw through saffron and gold
to an indifferent gray, a cold platinum,
a brutal blue; how he painted light's capacity
to nurture or wither, cell by cell.

Monody for Vincent van Gogh

If one draws a pollard willow as if it were a living being...
then the surroundings follow almost by themselves –
Vincent van Gogh, letter to brother Theo

In Arles, you tried to see
through *an eye more Japanese,*
how they drew with a *lightning flash.*
You complained your studies lacked
a certain *clearness of touch,* as if sight
inhabited your fingertips, in each whorl
a mildly cloudy eye. When heat blanched
the fields, you tried to catch *black notes*
in the landscape, since *any small darkness*
calls to me like water. The sun that scorched
in Arles followed you north, or the lightning
lived by then inside your head. Did you
relinquish light as your last experiment? A gun
is a small darkness. When it called to you,
you tried to see through a deader eye.

Dreaming on a Hard Mattress

I can never save him, my dream father
tumbling down an iron spiral staircase. Jerked
awake, I shudder like the metal struck
by an old man dropping. Or else, I lose him
in a canyon. He's hiking just ahead
but then he's not, and I am chasing
echoes. Once, he's climbing wide, white
steps while his legs forget
they no longer work. Before I can warn him,
he shouts for me; I'm swimming, frantic,
through the watery logic, knowing
when I reach him he'll be stiff as a starfish
on a bleached rock. But I never
reach him. Night after night he can't
rely on me. I'm lunging for him, pounding
doors, grabbling, stumbling, missing him
by inches; his dark eyes milking over,
his tongue getting thicker with my name.

"Cargador de Flores"

Diego Rivera, 1935
The Flower Carrier

It's him! In peasant whites and on all fours, pinned
under the weight of his towering wicker basket.
He stares at the floor of the museum like a mule,

this man who overlooked my childhood from a print
above my parents' bed. He's still burdened by blossoms
piled so high they shove his sombrero down over his brows.

As a girl, I admired the woman: how she leans
to adjust the basket that's fixed
to her man's back by a yellow sling.

Rivera draws my eye from the folds of the sling
to the folds in the woman's cream-colored shawl,
then upward to her lowered eyes.

My mother must have read love here
in all its colors, while my father saw
a laboring man knocked to his knees.

I can hear my father humming Spanish Civil War songs,
union hymns, choruses from battles
he would never risk his family to fight.

I can see my mother tugging up their bedspread,
securing its perfect daily crease with pillows,
as the painting keeps retelling old stories

about the loads of love: Of a man
who will never unshoulder his basket, of a woman
who will always be bending to help.

Of a wife who cannot keep herself from worrying
each knot tighter, a husband who wonders
how flowers turned heavy as stones.

Rummaging

She spends days rummaging
in that big black purse,
as if she's poking into dark
water, and coming up
with Kleenex, a wallet, I.D.s
she doesn't recognize.
She keeps finding and finding
the silver key marked
with red nail polish
so that she knows it goes
to the front door. Each time
she says, I'll have to mark
the front door key. All day,
she fingers the few small,
shiny things she's dredged:
freshman year, when the boys
elected her most popular
Radcliffe girl; her wedding day
and the rabbi's fishy eyes.
She worries odds and ends
to luster: a single earring;
a broken hearing aid; Anna,
Alex, Elad and those other two
great grandchildren whose names
she sometimes knows. She drags
the bag everywhere, even
as it empties of all but a few
glimmers, slippery to catch.

My Mother's Future, Named

Another morning in Dementia,
land of deep lakes
with confusing currents.

Dementia might be a star, rising late
in the winter sky. Or, how the *dementia*
twists as it flowers! Unstaked, a groping vine.

Slowly, Dementia will descend
the grand staircase. Clouds, lowering
to pour themselves over, and over.

Backstroking

My arms dig into the puddles of light.
The chlorine steam keeps rising.

Each breath I take, amplified by water,
still crashes against my eardrums.

But now, I stare up at some sky
that couldn't have been this elemental

blue two weeks ago, before my father
drifted from attachments.

Not that I picture him there above me,
lifeguarding from eternity.

There's just a difference
in the light I backstroke through –

where absence, newly angled,
reflects across flat water

and like water, changes all the colors,
textures, gravities.

When the sky ashes over, I think it couldn't
have been this gray two weeks ago.

This must be my father, tangled
in air he just swam through.

Two Ways

When I find a bird this morning
that's bashed itself
against my window, I think:

Viewed sparrow by sparrow,
death's not so unattractive.

No crosswind disturbs a feather.
Bird feet like twin starfish
curl, still attached to motion.

Now that the twittering's stopped
and the head's uncocked,
I can look straight into those eyes
that shine, and bother me like bees.

But by afternoon, ants nibble
every crumb of eye, devouring
last images. An ooze fixes
one skewed wing to earth.

This is another death,
sparrow unbecoming sparrow.
The chest collapses
as black ants swarm the heart.

Why We Don't Change Our Lives
or Move to Alaska

When we leave the park bus, a milky glacial river
beckons us nearer.

There are no trails. A sign directs:
Please spread out to spare the tundra.
Don't follow in anyone's footsteps.

We could wander caribou miles in any direction.

Summer on top of the world – daylight sprawls
into midnight. Even the caribou aren't in herds.

But habit leads us single-file
over monkshood, cow parsnip, geranium,
marsh marigold, into sparse-blooming shrub.

On a dwarf willow, we come across a tuft
that's not a flower – it might be coarse fur, snagged.

We pass the tuft between us until it's warm
as flesh, all thinking it's the same
dusty, carnivorous color as the grizzlies
we've watched through tour bus windows.

That's when we feel the massive sky
threatening, with its lumbering clouds; hear the river
growl from far away, ferocious with silt;

and retrace our steps to the ranger station,
remembering how they warn you not
to startle a grizzly – but if you do –

to wave your arms above your head
and calmly speak, so that the bear
does not mistake you for a caribou,
which wanders mutely, and with no imagination.

Yowl

True to his wolfish heart, that dog next door
bares his teeth, yips from his rooftop,

poised to jump me as if I'm a burglar
at my own gate. He's got it all:

territory and certainty; surefootedness,
not to mention lungs, to be a pack of one.

He also howls when I play jazz, his notes
outlasting John Coltrane's.

Sometimes I laugh and say, *that dog can swing*.

Sometimes I yell: *Dumb dog, how many years*
before you know where I belong?

But he just barks when I pull up, barks
as I'm unlocking my front door, until I fumble

like the stranger he knows I am. He's so sure
that I've come home to the wrong life.

I wonder if his ear can catch my true life swinging
somewhere else, improvising without me.

However long I live, it won't be long enough.
I'll still be longing, that same dumb human longing.

Next door, a different dog will bark.

II. History's Art

Venery

At the fish market: school, or make that shoal
of bass, lap of cod and glean of herrings.

A bind of salmon. Risk of lobsters, fever of rays.
Taint of tilapia, audience of squid, hover

of trout. Beds of clams and oysters, Manila
and Miyagi. Two different casts of crabs,

Dungeness, and small blue Chesapeakes
tipped back on ice so their cold eyes show.

Venery: the naming of groups.
Also the chasing of game, object of sport;

and from the Middle Ages, the pursuit
of sexual pleasure. Hunting, humping,

toying with collective nouns; all venery,
all the time, then, when life for gentlemen

was a rollicking ride to hounds. And the women,
did they come in a loveliness like ladybirds,

or a shiver like sharks? Mere business of ferrets
or troubling as goldfinches; with a lion's pride

or a zebra's dazzle? Leggy and lean giraffes,
some of them, at least, a journey?

Frontispiece, 1543

In their ignorance,
they thought
the human heart
had holes,
and in that dark
they could not enter
near the womb,
a woman's body hid
devilish instruments.

In the frontispiece
to his *De Corporus
Fabrica Humani*,
Vesalius has opened
the body of a woman.
He and a dozen students
read the corpse;
Renaissance men,
huddling, transfixed
by this new thrill, science,
as for the first time
light dissects her.

Vesalius scalpels
through the milky skin,
through the red to pearly
ligaments and bone.
Fingers descend
the marbled staircase
of her ribs, counting.
They limn the veins,

draw apart the tendons
where muscles meet,
expose God's craft.

An artist sketches
what's laid
                bare:

liver, lungs,
the heart which hides
no humors. Finally,
Vesalius cuts down
to the fibrous cradle
of hysteria called
uterus.

              There,
he holds the reeking
womb so they can see.
Physicians, artist,
students, all inspect
some lumps their eyes
infect with blame; agree
these must be Horns
of Venus; leave her
on the table – opened,
drawn, mislabeled.

History's Art

You'd think tracing would be true:
Brass rubbing. An impression
of one English knight buried in a church floor.

But design erodes, even etched in brass
on a flat stone. When you put paper to the grave
and press with a crayon made of cobbler's wax,
you're guessing blindly at those details lost
where people walk over centuries.

Pay attention to what stays sharp:
the spiky rowel of his spur, each long coarse hair
on the nape of the dog caught under his feet.

Or was that meant to be a conquered lion
symbolizing bravery? You only can imagine
his militant stink, the ferocious charging
of his heart beneath its armor.

Note his identity, heraldry, life history.
Then, what should you do about his wives –
their sole armorial bearings these brass plates;
their histories written nowhere but here,
where their loyalty's identically entombed?

The one to his right died in childbirth.
This one to his left, in childbirth.

Even after centuries, her headrest remains rigid
and unrevealing. The crayon gets the orbits
of her eyes, but leaves her pupils blank;
her straight nose is unremarkable
as that pious clasp of hands.

But when you rub her mouth
to bring out the distinctive pursing of her lips,
she comes alive. *I died too young*
on a blood-soaked bed, she says.
The rest is mostly lies.

To Lorine Niedecker

In every part of every living thing
is stuff that once was rock

Your elemental garden: rock and weed.
You worked it over, planting late and sparse
with mother, father, flowering granite seed.

In thickish air, you, booted to the knees,
caretaking to your father's speechless marsh,
your elemental garden: rock and weed.

And water always. Your paean place: the seas
that made us – mud where water grinds down quartz,
mother, father, flowering granite seed.

Such singular unearthing, such release
of power from the stone, the stem, the splash.
No ornamental garden: rock and weed.

Suggest my stone bare elements to me.
Where do I muck for my refrain, what harsh
mother, father, flowering granite seed?

Rooting where the backwater meets the deep
(that shifty place with barely room to perch),
your elemental garden: rock and weed,
mother, father. Flowering granite seed.

September Birthday

For my father

Time for me to put on your worn gray sweater
and button it. It's autumn,

when the sky drops closer to the earth.
You lie three years under.

I'd like to think by now you are a tree
starting, and someday will bear apples.

But you are ashes boxed and buried – nothing more
than your dead cigars. Not even smoke can rise from you.

I mean to wrap my memories in heavy flannel,
store them away. But I have no trunk, no cedar chest.

They're like your sweater in my closet – something
I push aside each morning to dress for work.

I haven't put a single pebble on your grave.
I wait, instead, for you to visit me.

I don't count the midnight rustling
in the ivy, which I know is deer.

But because you are nowhere
and everywhere at once, I did wonder

about a bird that fluttered strangely
just now at my window – how it looked

through the glass, would not fly away,
then did.

Survival

Even a samovar
that rode the boat
with my grandmother, vanished
like the *shtetl* world
it came from, up in smoke
as if its nickel and its lead
were no harder
or more permanent
than a shoe box crammed
with photos of the long-dead;
than table linens
that had been my mother's
cross-stitched dowry;
than oil paintings
that hung for years, then
ran at the first lick
of heat. When fire tore
their house down
to the foundation, it erased
every item my parents owned
from six decades of marriage
– except one
small Wedgwood dish,
blue and heart-shaped.
I found the dish intact
where flames had whipped
2000 hardbound books
into creamy ash,
but my parents didn't want it.
They'd already started over.
I won't claim I saved it;

I just took the heart
for my mantelpiece.
What saved it was
the ferocious heat
at which Wedgwood bakes
to hardness.

Immigrant

Science can't convince me
I'm not related to this snowy egret
who reminds me of my grandmother.

Hunched like a widow's back, feathered
like a vintage hat, she picks her way
across a pebbly beach and toes the water.

Any moment she might speak,
stern and guttural, ask me if I brought
a "bath costume" for the beach –

pronounced as *bishh*. And I will say
the least I can, shying from conversation
with creatures alien and weathered.

I won't understand enough to pity her
the cold, brittle home she makes.
Only later – when I consider

the distance that she flew here
without knowing where she'd land –
will I call it deftness, call it courage.

To Yiddish

I heard on the radio that you're dying.
They're studying you in colleges
like a bird in a tray. Scholars will pick at you
with tweezers, while your ruddy feathers dull
to the color of long-dried blood. They'll debate
how your song sounded as the sun came up
in Lodz, Kovno, Kiev…

Peddling bread. Pleading for mercy.
Clamoring down an alley after *shul*.
Chiding a *meydla* not to fidget
while her thick hair is tugged into braids.
Whispering on warm, sleepy tongues...

One grandmother left you on the boat.
She was fourteen and alone, bearing the weight
of a samovar and brass candlesticks.

Her mother came later, too old to learn
even a greenhorn's English, and made poems
from you that her grandchildren couldn't read.

At least my mother listened.
She remembers lonely phrases,
how her *bubbe* recited poems
that sounded like dirges...

I should have made you my mother tongue,
then begged for your stories.
Now no children gather round you.

Awake at night in California, I'll wonder:
was that wind rattling the eucalyptus leaves
or your last words I heard?

At the National Holocaust Museum

Whichever word you speak –
you owe to destruction – Paul Celan

He herds his two daughters to the glass,
begins in his museum voice, that declaratory
read-aloud he'd use for Stone Age Tools
or the Habitat of Bees: *Majdanek Table.*

His girls stand level with a table;
here bodies splayed, opened
for gold or diamonds. If the girls could read,
a sign would tell them: "blood drained
through a central hole."

He looks at this display and probes
its photographs, its implements,
for ordinary words that, melted down,
can be reused.

Oven. Table. Tooth.

It might be a kitchen scene.

He clears his throat, finds a candied voice
for spooning facts into his children:
Look, that's the stretcher!

But there's no hope of rescue here,
no metaphor, not even adjectives
in the sign that says this "stretcher
moved corpses into ovens."

He sees that he's confused them, that he's confused
the stretcher, which is somewhere else,
with a twisted metal rack that camp guards
named a "roast" – a truck chassis
guards stacked with flesh, then lit.

The heat from so much burning fat warped steel.
How could language stand a chance?

He remains determined, though,
to attach the right word to the right device.

He's finding his voice in this matter of fact –

No, that's the stretcher over there –

when his girls run off ahead, their patent leather
tattooing past the piles of shoes, the suitcases,
in and out of the boxcar.

Pantoum of The Blue Virgin

(and 150 windows of Chartres)

What shatters cannot be restored. In two world wars,
men climbed close to Christ, his honeyed robes, his milky face;
pried out every pane that lit the cold cathedral floors;
unseated Mary's babe, each angel and each dove, to keep them safe.

Men climbed close to Christ, his honeyed robes, his milky face.
To spare medieval miracles from modern bombs,
they crated Mary's babe, each angel and each dove, to keep them safe.
The workmen must have trembled like palms.

To spare medieval miracles from modern bombs,
the jewels that had (by grace of God, some said) endured,
workmen must have trembled like palms,
and wondered what would continue as before.

The jewels that had (by grace of God, some said) endured
were stashed unseen, in the countryside.
What would continue as before?
How many times would The Blue Virgin hide

unseen in the countryside
where each village names those it lost in wars for France.
How many times would The Blue Virgin hide
swaddled piece by piece, nothing left to chance.

Each village names, unlucky son by son, those lost to France.
Men pried every pane that lit the cold cathedral floors,
swaddled piece by piece, left no thing to chance
in two world wars. What shatters cannot be restored.

Outside, the World

Screech owls bring small blind snakes to their nests and release
them to feed, reducing the number of insects who compete for
headless mice and other tidbits the owls cache.

Snug under my quilt, I don't want to think
about a field mouse hunkered in dry grass
or the owl set to tear the tasty meat
of its body from the tastier meat of its head.

So I can't love this screecher, whose shriek
rips through my night and scrapes the screen
off darkness – where animals are
on the hunt and always hungry.

Each screech demands its answer.
Outside, the world continues
to divide itself. I did love a hoot owl,
though, that once nested in our cedar.

It would gently ask me *who*, but never
forced me to choose sides, did not disrupt
domestic dreaming to remind me
there's suffering in the underbrush

and annihilation wherever history picks
who is to be the thrashing mouse, who
the implacable beak. It never seemed to ask
what have you done to deserve your bed.

I am the small blind snake
whisked on a chilling flight, no choice but
to let itself be carried. Just when hope
dwindles, left as far below as loam,

the snake finds itself alive, dumped
into a grub-stocked feathered nest.
Clueless at the turn that fortune took.
Bellying up to make the best of it.

III. Body and Soul

Courting the Rogue Wave

From the safety of the parking lot, you and I
agree they're dumb – that couple scuttling
along a rocky finger while winter surf
thrashes all around them.

A red-coated woman leads, aiming
for the finger's tip where wave after
gunmetal wave lifts to hammer boulders.
The man takes out his camera.

                         Stupid,
we decide as always – to go beyond
the yellow tape at the cliff's restless edge,
trip past a sign that warns how one
rogue wave can wrench somebody

out of the snug socket of his life.
But are you also thinking about thunder
at their feet, the way spray whips up
blood to the surface of the skin?

Do you half hope, too – as we watch them
lean into the center of the roar –
that a giant wave sneaks into their picture
to prove how stupid, truly stupid, they are?

Tenor

A dull case opened to red plush
and inside, the golden tongue –

my son's first saxophone. I fell in love
with flatted fifths, bent notes,

new vocabulary of quick licks,
scales and modes he learned to solo

over chords, covering the changes.
Once a boy who couldn't catch his breath,

then a man who punched it into riffs.
Isn't each child a lesson in some art?

Twice, I took breathing classes to give birth.
But no one taught me mourning

would begin the instant they met air,
their unmerciful progressions.

As my son learned to trust his lungs,
I tried to master circular breathing –

at the same time taking in
and letting go – a musician's trick

for the long held note finally released
so the next one can be caught.

Body and Soul

(Coleman Hawkins)

He played cello first, gripped it
between his knees and drew
his slow bow across until
he fell in love with moaning.
But flanks and hands
were not enough, he had to touch
the music's brassy body
with his tongue.

On 52nd St., they didn't know
a saxophone could speak
until Hawk made it reedy,
throaty, salty, bitter
sweet for them. That man
could swirl their smoke, squeeze
a note until their whiskey sloshed.
He could make honey sting
and gravel sing.

Some nights
people thought he dug
so deep no one else
could ever fill the hole.

He'd go home, put on
Debussy and Ravel.

Other tenors fingered faster,
swung wilder, bopped brighter,
but Hawk was first
to mouth that sax until despair
slurred
          to desire
and the music sobbed,
trembled like strings.

The punishment

for inattention can be forever, so the man sprinting
through the parking lot and shouting *Alistair!*
trailed by a grocery clerk who asks

do you think he could have come out here?
is living a Please-God-No moment until someone
spots his two year old in the bread aisle.

Young father, white-faced
and raw, reunites with Alistair
who's sweetly sucking on a juice straw.

I could tell him: the near-misses
will accrue, they all weigh. Every time
you turn your back on the ocean.

I could warn him, as my pulse
begins to settle: that thump against your ribs
is the extra heart new parents grow.

Even old, vestigial, it may jump –
pony trained by years of moments
when the worst could have been your fault.

But he's clutching Alistair and, adrenaline-
pumped voice too loud on the cell phone,
telling his wife that in the scramble

of his day, he let their child go
for four or five *really freaky minutes* ...
needing to confess his inattention,

and that he got away with it.

Happiness

She's peeling a pepper's red meat
away from its charred skin when she stops
to admire what she's made so soft and sweet
by roasting. Now that the pepper no longer
resembles an un-bruised heart, she likes it
even more. She knows herself: that she withstands
joy as well as pain, that she quibbles
with her good luck, often can't see through
a day's gray skin. Lines around her mouth
turn down. Total strangers feel obliged
to remind her to smile. But she enjoys
picking off every fleck of char, imagining
how good this pepper will taste to those
she loves: almost sugary. She dumps burned bits
in the trash, and slices the bright red flesh
into tender strips. Even one small bite
is too good to throw away.

Our Geology

On this new map, the creek
behind our house runs red.

Our slope lush with ivy,
avocado, acacia and bay laurel,
hides an active earthquake fault.

Here –
give or take
a few yards east or west – we sit
on the edge of being ripped apart:

Where we grind our morning coffee,
sleep on a high blue bed
we never finished painting.
Where we made life together,
hung our children's handprints,
their graduation photos.
Where we fell, broke, healed,
held.

We're not any more exposed today
than yesterday.

But now our faultline's marked.

An ending, mapped.

Aubade

At five, I lie and listen
to our house, how quiet mounts
stairs that used to clomp with kids.

As I think – these days
we wouldn't even have to close
the bedroom door – your hands find
my lower back, circle
where they know the knots are.
By now, a thought can wake
and stir the air between us.

Your fingers, warm and slow
from recent dreaming, stick lightly
to my skin as they begin
around my hips. But they pause, then
drop; I catch the sudden lisp
in breath that means you've drifted off.

Dozing, I wake again at eight. You've left
the *New York Times* and coffee
in my favorite mug beside our bed.
It's no longer steaming hot
but warm, still good.

Of the Body

Fresh death
pulled turkey buzzards down
from their high wheeling. Six ripped
the carcass of a lamb as other sheep
continued their woolly milling about the field
without a bleat of mourning or alarm.

A few yards away,
farmhouse windows were happy with light
and cars moved casually towards the coast
while the buzzards in their huddle, awful
and almost human, sorted themselves
around their table. Dug in with beaks and feet.

Gregarious,
hunched in black, they could have been *Chassids*,
or any prayerful circle gathered round
some sacred hunger; anatomists
unraveling the mystery of the body;
old, bald philosophers in frock coats.

Did I imagine
they radiated buzzardly contentment,
joy? They were only turkey vultures,
each wattle-colored head an ugly watch cap
over a primitive brain, no shame
in their allotted appetites.

Honest
in their hunger, they were brazen
and unhurried: One drank at an eye
while another tugged a bloody sinew.
I watched their red heads bob
into the belly.

Not one
existential theory passed between them.
I left and couldn't look again
until they'd done exposing death
bare-boned – until I knew the sun
had begun its bleaching.

To a Young Hacker

R.I.P. Josh

Want to hear about your funeral?
Only the hole in the ground was willing.
Two workers, kneeling at your head and feet,
lowered your pine box into earth – and froze
as their electric sling kept refusing
to release you. Their red faces wept
with sweat. One worker jerked a strap,
and you knocked against your coffin,
lurched in the bottom of your grave.
Even the rabbi faltered at the thud.
Grief itself stopped breathing – paralyzed
by a sudden vision of you about to rise
to trouble-shoot the problem. Alive,
you couldn't pass a locked door
without attempting to invent a key; or
ignore any button that might be pushed
just to see what happened next.
Somehow you hacked into eternity
years and years too soon.
For that moment when you stuck,
suspended, we let ourselves believe:
if anyone could, it would be you
who figured out the angles,
relit your eyes, resumed your mischief.
When you settled down, instead,
we flung clods the size of fists
that pounded on your lid.

Carousel Designer, 75

"A master of whimsy whose painted steeds romped worldwide." – *The New York Times*

He sculpted manes to look alive
as wings, necks muscled from exertions
of lifetimes going nowhere.

He made his horses fight their bits
of gold, their tongues thrust
to scream or nicker.

As if his steeds might burst across
real grasslands, he captured them
in constant flight.

That's how he mastered whimsy,
contained it, so it couldn't canter off
into wild laughter.

He trapped them all in gilt, but loved
his jumpers most: those he plunged
up and down the relentless worlds

he stuck them in. As he engineered
delight, perhaps he also mastered
sorrow. It followed him around,

but gave way sometimes to whimsy
which would whinny up
to lick the sugar off his palm.

The Most You Can Hope For

Wanting and dissatisfaction
are the main ingredients
of happiness – Ruth Stone, "Wanting"

Mix salt of tears, salt of the sea-womb, salt
of blood lively with your pulse.

For fidelity, snip rosemary. Crush
till pungent with pining. Add sweet basil,

because the Mediterranean is only semi-arid,
which may be the most you can hope for.

Pick a lemon that's brilliant, avoid the palest
yellow of caution or cowardice. Sugar it –

you're after the sweet and sour taste
of contradiction on your tongue.

You're making hope, which won't exist
without dissatisfaction. You're making life,

which fattens on hope. Avoid blandness,
avoid bitterness. When you're making happiness:

Don't ever stop to test for doneness.

IV. Next Time

Rewriting *War and Peace*

Kapli kapali – "Drops dripped"
is the shortest sentence in *War and Peace*

Fall fell.
Drops dripped.

Armies armed.
Battalions battled.

Shooters shot.
Boys bayoneted

          Boys,
Bayoneted. Blades
Bled. Drops dripped.
Dogs dined.

Mothers mourned.
Wives wept.
Drops dripped.

Fall fell.
Men manned.
Armies swarmed
Like flies.

Like flies.

Sherlock Holmes' Darkest Hour

I offer up my abracadabra of the intellect, and they believe
I can distinguish footprints of a cleric maimed in Borneo
from a clerk lamed in Brighton. They come for answers

when one man crumples in his country house, but
children in an East End alley die among the sweepings,
unanswered for. I decipher trifling mysteries,

give people Moriarty to blame instead of God.
Elementary. While the cause of Evil continues
to elude me like an echo. Who masterminds

an echo? What could explain our genius
for justifying deaths? Oh Watson, you ask
why I pace my chamber, fixing myself

with cocaine's cotton clarity and confidence;
you scold me when I wallow in white powder
and my violin's cold tremolo.

But I cannot keep feeding the world's addiction
to explanation. I, the greatest detector of murder
in all guises – slabbering hound, swarthy traveler, asp

snaking down the braided bell pull – must smother
my own doubts, the way that voices choke tonight
on Baker Street, die in this bituminous fog.

Iraq War Blues

Once, I saw a dog drowning in a reservoir.
        He barked and swam in circles, out deep,
                his brown head barely above water.

I watched from the lake's tall granite rim
        as a man held out a branch then chucked it
                close to shore. People called, *Here, Boy,*

though no one seemed to know his name
        or how he came there. A woman clucked
                her tongue, encouraged him

with soothing noises, commanded him
        with whistles. His shrill bark argued back.
                He was stuck in a circular logic –

fear, probably. Or he'd clamped down
        on one slim stick of a belief
                and could not let it go.

His pumping legs and heart
        might even have convinced him
                that he was getting somewhere,

like people who are determined
        but self-defeating. As I walked away,
                his barking made the rocks toll

and trailed after me still arguing
        that with no amount of effort
                could I ever change his mind.

No amount of effort would ever change
        his mind. His barking, though,
                trailed after me still arguing.

Mother's Day Gift

For my daughter

As I admire these irises
that you brought, forgive me.
I picture how soon they'll drop,

blue petal by petal, all pretense
that they can live forever
in a shapely vase. Good daughter,

I'm sorry in advance for that day
when love's duties grow old,
no longer small or pretty.

I know that you will feed me
your angers mixed with love,
just as I have spooned

my own mother her pills,
bitter tablets crushed
in such sweet apple sauce.

Night After the Funeral

For my mother

Geese announce themselves
near daybreak; no need to look up
to picture the arrow they aim north.

We may envy their wildness,
their life without lanes
as they fly over our pavements,

our roofs and wrecks, honking
themselves hoarse. Peddlers
of a tired freedom,

they are bound by seasons
and the urgency
in their DNA, just like us.

For once, flight holds no charm.
Death makes distance
lose its attraction.

Being lighter than air
is an illusion, as is escape.
No wings are fast enough.

Round in Memory of the Children of Minamisanriku*

in the *shush* of waves, your wheels

refuse to stop their motion

pedal faster

dusk is now forever after

no one calls you in for meals

your home is ocean

in the *shush* of waves, your wheels

in the *shush* of waves, your wheels

refuse to stop their motion

pedal faster

dusk is now forever after

no one calls you in for meals

your home is ocean

in the *shush* of waves, your wheels

*Minamisanriku was a Japanese village washed away by tsunami on March 11, 2011.

Playful Abstract Painter, 79

"'You need to look at a painting with the tongue of your eye,' he was known to say."

New York Times obituary of Robert Natkin

Once, he licked a Vermeer at the Frick
to taste the colors.

At the Art Institute of Chicago, tongue
in cheek, he swiped a Poussin off the wall

and hung a canvas of his own. No one noticed.
People can be tasteless, meaning blind.

His mother worked and worried
in the garment trade. She knew colors

don't put food onto a table, so demanded
the art teacher hand her son an F.

Art school preached: mix yellow, blue, and red
instead of black. But he used black, delicious

as night's licorice, as charred crumbs
from the last crust of bread, as water

when it's poured into the coldest, deepest
pool of rock. Some called him a poet –

and poets also roll the many flavors
of light across the tongue.

In later years, his work out of favor, he heard
the voices of his paintings fill his studio.

They too, it seemed, had mouths.
He said they shouted victory or defeat.

He'd tasted both and lived on very little,
but his eyes were always fed.

Beginning Birding

Before I found its page among the passerines,
I'd never seen a Black Phoebe.

I learned its family name means Tyrant Flycatcher;
and there it was outside my window, bullying insects!

It sallied off a phone wire – cursive flights
to make each midair snatch. The next day, too,

I saw one in the yard: sooty and white;
twitchy-tailed and crested. It said: *seek, seek.*

I saw another one next door, and when I strolled,
a Phoebe followed me gate to gate.

Black Phoebes waited everywhere I looked,
that obscure word you learn – then notice daily.

Though birds have no need to be written,
I felt I'd called Phoebes into being

from an alphabet of feather and full throttle.
How quickly it becomes about possession.

Soon, I was naming more birds into sight:
Let there be Bewick's Wrens and Hairy Woodpeckers;

Rufous-sided Towhees, Yellow-rumped Warblers.
Let there be Sharp-shinned Hawks!

Spousely-Held

I'll put down that it's spousely-held —
mortgage broker

Even after I no longer want
to be arousely-held, love,
I'll want to be spousely-held.

When I don't need to be Wowsly-held,
I'll still need to be sousely-held, clutched
to your chest like a bottle

that can't be pried from your grip. Hold me
for years yet, until I'm so short of breath that breath
stops short, and I die housely-held in your arms.

Then burn me, bag me, box me, shelf me.
Say a few kind words. I'll wait
patient as only ash can be patient,

my objections to death mousely-held.
I want our ashes to float in the ocean,
wrapping, a cloud in the water

suspended in waves. Let's be unsettled
as salt, and drift off a pier where we sat
when we were vowsly-held.

Thanksgiving Day

I know the world's a cruel mess and I apologize
that when today's low autumn sun lit
our fire maple's leaves, it made me unreasonably happy.

When wind gusted and set a school of five-pointed shadows
swimming across our room in a wash of gold, I smiled,
and loved my eyes. There's plenty of time later to be blind

to beauty that fills one small window, a riot of red
that isn't bloody, green that doesn't smack
of anybody's army. Another day, I'll ignore an orange blaze

if it's not a torched and flaming car, or any yellow too innocent
to cordon off a crime scene. But the maple colors flared, so alive
in late afternoon that, for awhile, I didn't even think

tomorrow this wind will rip away these leaves. Incandescence
will be guttered and the tree will bare its skeleton, but today
its rushing colors made me laugh out loud – grateful

for the beauty of a moment with no winners, no losers,
no complicity – thankful for those instants that occur
before thought can complicate delight.

The Woman Who Feels No Fear

Doctors have reported that a brain anomaly left a woman without fear.

She pets scorpions and snarling dogs. Lightning fails
      to torch her nerves. Let the elevator plunge –
          nothing makes her organs lurch.

She cooks with butter, dives into the deep end.
      We envy her – no spear in the heart,
          no hornets in the gut

when her little girl is hours late and sirens shriek.
      She'll never turn a small dark mole
          into a malignant mountain. Though,

if she lives long, it's because death is just another bully
      who doesn't know what to do with her: woman
          immune to wolves outside the tent.

And how she struts onto any stage, life of the party,
      always game, flips off the boss or flirts with him
          in the presence of his wife.

If we met her, we'd gather round, as if she lives
      in a land-locked country and we must tell her
          how it feels to be at sea.

We'd clutch our cocktails and inspect her eyes
      for vacancy, as if she's less like us than a dog is
          who puddles every time there's thunder.

Does she look upon the rest of us with mercy
        or do we baffle her – the way we knock on wood,
                our sweaty bargains with gods we half-believe in?

The army is interested in her brain. But as torturer she'd lack
        imagination, not knowing what makes people shiver
                besides the cold. Surely, she must feel the cold.

Next Time

As I was batting around the ball
of an idea, it turned into a bird –

unfolded – the way I hope
a poem unfolds and startles me.

I'd like to be a bird next time.
Birds don't need to learn

to love the world. Gray sky
is a stone any bird can enter.

Or, I'll be a black-eyed seal
that breaks the surface, shiny

with news of its deeper life –
the way I hope to come back

as a poem that surfaces,
re-surfaces, keeps glistening.

Acknowledgments

I'd like to thank the publications where the following poems appeared, sometimes in different versions or under different titles:

Journals:
Alehouse: "Our Geology"; *Atlanta Review*: "Mother's Day Gift,""The Woman Who Feels No Fear"; *Broadsided*: "Round in Memory of the Children of Minamisanriku"(as "Minamisanriku Child"); *California Quarterly*: "Monody for Vincent Van Gogh"; *CALYX*: "Immigrant"; *Connecticut Review*: "My Mother's Future, Named"; *New Millennium Writings*: "Survival"; *Nimrod*: "Lucky Dog"; *Oberon*: "Venery"; *Passager*: "Spousely-held"; *Poetry East*: "Beginning Birding" (later in *Canary*), "Happiness,""Next Time"; *Poetry International*: "At the National Holocaust Museum," "Backstroking"; *Poet Lore*: "Dreaming on a Hard Mattress,""At the X-Ray Clinic "(later in *Ekphrasis*); *Puerto del Sol*: "Why We Don't Change Our Lives or Move to Alaska"; *River Styx:* "Pantoum of the Blue Virgin"; *Seattle Review*: "Chamber Music,""Yowl" (as "Dog Years"); *Southern Poetry Review*: "Cargador de Flores"; *Sow's Ear Poetry Review*: "Throat Singing"; *Spillway*: "Rummaging"; *Tar River Poetry*: "Aubade," "Body and Soul" (as "Coleman Hawkins"); *Tucumcari Review*: "To Lorine Niedecker".

Anthologies:
Dogs Singing: A Tribute Anthology (Salmon Poetry): "Yowl"
From the Well of Living Waters (Kehilla Community Synagogue): "To Yiddish"; "Thanksgiving Day"

Marin Poetry Center Anthology 2008: "September Birthday"
Marin Poetry Center Anthology 2009: "Carousel Designer, 75"
Marin Poetry Center Anthology 2010: "To a Young Hacker"
Marin Poetry Center Anthology 2011: "Under Trees"
Turning a Train of Thought Upside Down: An Anthology of Women's Poetry (Scarlet Tanager Books): "Cargador de Flores," "Chamber Music".

Chapbooks:
Backstroking (Unfinished Monument Press): "Frontispiece, 1543"; "History's Art"; "To Yiddish"; "Under Trees"; "Two Ways" (later on *Verse Daily*); "Sherlock Holmes' Darkest Hour".
Finding the Sweet Spot (Finishing Line Press): "Iraq War Blues" (as "Memoir of an Innocent Bystander"); "Thanksgiving Day".

Thank you to those who awarded these poems honors: "The Woman Who Feels No Fear," 2011 Rita Dove Poetry Prize from Salem College's Center for Women Writers and International Publication Prize from *Atlanta Review*; "Lucky Dog," finalist 2011 *Nimrod*/Pablo Neruda Prize; "Pantoum for the Blue Virgin," 2010 International Poetry Contest winner *River Styx* (honorable mention); "Survival," Best Poem Award from *New Millennium Writings*. *Backstroking* won the Acorn-Rukeyser Chapbook Award from Mekler & Deahl Publishers. An earlier version of this manuscript was a finalist, under the title *Dreaming on a Hard Mattress*, for the 2010 Ashland Press Richard Snyder Award and the ABZ First Book Prize.

About the Author

Susan Cohen has been a newspaper reporter, a professor at the University of California Graduate School of Journalism, and a contributing writer to the *Washington Post Magazine*. Since spending a year on a John S. Knight Fellowship at Stanford University, where she divided her time between studying bioethics and poetry, she's authored two chapbooks of poems as well as co-authored a non-fiction book. Her poems have won the Acorn-Rukeyser Chapbook Award, the Rita Dove Poetry Award from Salem College's Center for Women Writers, a Best Poem Award from *New Millennium Writings*, and recognition from *Arts & Letters*, *Atlanta Review*, *Nimrod*, *River Styx*, and other journals. Her work has been anthologized in collections from Salmon Poetry and City Works Press and nominated for a Pushcart Prize. Also a two-time winner of the Science in Society Award from the National Association of Science Writers, the mother of two, and a beginning birder, she lives in Berkeley with her husband.

Printed in Great Britain
by Amazon